EMMANUEL JOSEPH

Digital Body Language, What Your Clicks, Pauses, and Emojis Are Really Saying

First edition

This book was professionally typeset on Reedsy.
Find out more at reedsy.com

Contents

1

Chapter 1

START OFF

Digital Body Language: What Your Clicks, Pauses, and Emojis Are Really Saying unveils the hidden signals we send every day through screens. Blending linguistics, behavioral psychology, tech culture, and modern relationships, this book decodes the unspoken grammar of the digital age—from the suspense of the typing indicator to the intimacy of emojis, the sting of ghosting, and the subtle power of scrolling. It makes the virtual feel viscerally personal, showing how our online gestures shape trust, intimacy, and identity. With sharp insights and relatable stories, it reveals that every click, pause, and emoji is more than a habit—it's a language of connection, desire, and meaning in our hyperconnected world.

Keywords

digital communication; online behavior; tech culture; emojis; ghosting; social media psychology; digital intimacy; typing indicator; online presence; scrolling habits; relationship dynamics; behavioral psychology; digital trust; virtual identity; digital body language

2

Chapter 1: The Silent Grammar of Screens

Digital communication has created a new grammar, one that doesn't rely on spoken words but on pauses, clicks, and subtle cues. When you hesitate before replying, that silence becomes a sentence in itself. It tells the other person you are weighing your words, distracted, or perhaps emotionally conflicted. Unlike spoken language, where tone and body gestures fill the gaps, digital silence is stark and often over-interpreted. The absence of a reply can feel louder than any message.

This grammar is shaped by the platforms we use. A pause on WhatsApp, where "typing..." appears, feels different from a pause on email, where no such indicator exists. The anticipation of response becomes part of the communication itself. People project meaning into these gaps, often revealing more about their own insecurities than the sender's intent.

Clicks, too, are part of this grammar. The act of opening a message but not replying is a gesture akin to turning your head away in a conversation. It signals acknowledgment without engagement. In relationships, this can be interpreted as disinterest, avoidance, or simply busyness. The digital grammar is unforgiving because it lacks the warmth of human presence.

Understanding this silent grammar requires us to rethink how we interpret intent. Just as linguists study pauses in speech, we must study pauses in digital interaction. They are not empty spaces but loaded signals, shaping how intimacy, trust, and misunderstanding unfold in the digital age.

3

Chapter 2: The Psychology of the Typing Indicator

Few digital cues are as psychologically charged as the typing indicator. That flickering ellipsis is a promise of words yet to come, a suspenseful pause that can heighten anticipation or anxiety. It is the digital equivalent of someone inhaling before speaking.

Behavioral psychology explains why this matters: humans are wired to anticipate completion. When we see "typing...," our brains prepare for closure. If the message arrives quickly, relief follows. If it lingers, tension builds. And if it disappears without a message, frustration or paranoia can set in.

In relationships, the typing indicator becomes a mirror of emotional investment. A partner who types for long stretches before sending a short reply may be seen as withholding, while someone who fires off quick responses may be perceived as casual or careless. These interpretations often say more about the receiver's expectations than the sender's intent.

The typing indicator is a reminder that digital body language is not neutral. It manipulates our psychology, shaping how we feel about conversations and the people behind them. It is a small design choice with profound emotional consequences.

4

Chapter 3: Emojis as Emotional Dialects

Emojis are not mere decorations; they are dialects of digital emotion. A smiley face can soften criticism, while a heart can transform a mundane message into intimacy. They function as tone markers, filling the void left by the absence of facial expressions and vocal inflections.

Linguistically, emojis operate like punctuation. They signal mood, intent, and emphasis. A sentence ending with a period may feel cold, but add a wink emoji and it becomes playful. This shift in meaning shows how emojis have become integral to digital grammar.

Psychologically, emojis allow people to express emotions they might struggle to articulate. A crying-laughing face can mask discomfort, while a flame emoji can signal attraction without words. They are shorthand for complex feelings, reducing vulnerability while maintaining connection.

Yet emojis are culturally coded. A peach may mean fruit in one context and sexuality in another. Misinterpretations abound, especially across generations. Understanding emojis requires not just linguistic awareness but cultural sensitivity, making them one of the most fascinating aspects of digital body language.

5

Chapter 4: The Pause That Speaks Volumes

In digital communication, pauses are magnified. A delay in response can feel like rejection, indifference, or deep thought. Unlike face-to-face pauses, which are fleeting, digital pauses stretch across minutes, hours, or days, leaving room for endless speculation.

Psychologists note that humans are prone to "negative fill-in"—assuming the worst when information is missing. A delayed reply often triggers insecurity, especially in relationships. The pause becomes a canvas onto which fears and hopes are projected.

But pauses can also be strategic. In professional settings, delaying a reply can signal authority or careful consideration. In personal contexts, it can create suspense or test commitment. The meaning of a pause depends on the relationship and the stakes involved.

Ultimately, pauses remind us that silence is not neutral. In digital spaces, it is a powerful form of body language, shaping trust, intimacy, and conflict in ways we are only beginning to understand.

6

Chapter 5: The Double-Tap and Its Hidden Meanings

The double-tap "like" on social media is deceptively simple. It appears as a gesture of approval, but its meanings are layered. A like can signal genuine appreciation, obligatory politeness, or subtle flirtation.

Behavioral psychology shows that likes trigger dopamine, reinforcing both the sender and receiver. The act of liking becomes a ritual of validation, shaping self-esteem and social dynamics.

In relationships, likes can be loaded. A partner liking an ex's photo may spark jealousy, while liking a friend's achievement may strengthen bonds. The ambiguity of the gesture makes it fertile ground for misinterpretation.

The double-tap is digital applause, but also digital surveillance. It reveals where attention goes, exposing desires and loyalties. In this way, it is both a gift and a risk, shaping how intimacy and trust are negotiated online.

7

Chapter 6: Ghosting as Digital Disappearance

Ghosting is the ultimate act of digital body language: silence as severance. It is not just the absence of words but the withdrawal of presence. To be ghosted is to experience a digital death of connection.

Psychologically, ghosting exploits the ambiguity of digital communication. Unlike face-to-face rejection, which is explicit, ghosting leaves the receiver in limbo. The lack of closure intensifies pain, as the mind struggles to make sense of the silence.

Ghosting reflects tech culture's emphasis on convenience. Ending a relationship with a click avoids confrontation but sacrifices empathy. It is a symptom of a culture that values efficiency over emotional responsibility.

Yet ghosting also reveals vulnerability. Those who ghost often fear conflict or lack emotional tools to navigate endings. It is not just cruelty but avoidance, a digital defense mechanism that speaks volumes about modern relationships.

8

Chapter 7: The Psychology of Seen Messages

The "seen" receipt is one of the most charged signals in digital communication. It confirms presence but not engagement. To know someone has read your words but chosen not to reply is a uniquely modern form of rejection.

Behavioral psychology explains why this stings: humans equate acknowledgment with obligation. When someone sees a message, we expect reciprocity. The absence of reply violates this expectation, triggering feelings of neglect.

In professional contexts, seen receipts can signal efficiency or dismissal. In personal contexts, they can breed insecurity or resentment. The meaning depends on the relationship and the emotional stakes.

Seen receipts are digital eye contact. They confirm awareness but deny response, creating a tension that defines much of modern communication.

9

Chapter 8: The Language of Notifications

Notifications are the whispers of the digital world. Each ping, buzz, or badge is a call for attention, shaping how we prioritize relationships and tasks. They are not neutral; they are designed to provoke action.

Psychologists note that notifications exploit the brain's reward system. The unpredictability of alerts creates a slot-machine effect, keeping us hooked. This shapes not just behavior but emotional rhythms.

In relationships, notifications can become battlegrounds. A partner's irritation at delayed replies often stems from the assumption that notifications are instant. The expectation of immediacy reshapes intimacy, making patience a rare commodity.

Notifications are the soundtrack of digital life. They dictate when we engage, how we feel, and what we value, making them central to the study of digital body language.

Chapter 9: The Subtext of Screenshots

Screenshots are digital artifacts of trust and betrayal. They can preserve affection or expose secrets. To be screenshotted is to have your words frozen, stripped of context, and potentially weaponized.

Psychologically, screenshots reflect control. They allow one party to capture and curate reality, often without consent. This power dynamic shapes how people communicate, knowing their words may be preserved.

In friendships, screenshots can be playful—sharing memes or jokes. In conflicts, they can be destructive, used to shame or manipulate. The act of capturing is itself a form of body language, signaling intent.

Screenshots remind us that digital communication is never ephemeral. Every word can be archived, making trust both fragile and essential in the digital age.

11

Chapter 10: The Rhythm of Scrolling

Scrolling is the heartbeat of digital life. The speed, pauses, and stops reveal attention and desire. A quick scroll suggests disinterest, while lingering signals curiosity or attraction.

Behavioral psychology shows that scrolling patterns reflect mood. Restless scrolling may indicate boredom or anxiety, while deliberate scrolling suggests focus. Platforms design feeds to exploit these rhythms, keeping users engaged.

In relationships, scrolling can become a source of conflict. A partner's scrolling during conversation may feel like neglect, while scrolling through someone's profile can signal obsession. The act itself is a language of attention.

Scrolling is not passive. It is a gesture that reveals priorities, shaping how intimacy, curiosity, and distraction coexist in the digital age.

12

Chapter 11: The Subtle Power of Status Updates

Status updates are declarations of digital presence. They are not just information but signals of identity, mood, and belonging. A vague post can invite speculation, while a detailed one can assert control over narrative.

Psychologically, status updates function as self-presentation. They allow individuals to curate how they are perceived, blending authenticity with performance. The act of posting is itself a gesture of visibility.

In relationships, status updates can be loaded. A cryptic message may spark concern or jealousy, while a celebratory post can strengthen bonds. The ambiguity of updates makes them fertile ground for interpretation.

Status updates are digital stagecraft. They reveal not just what we say but how we want to be seen, shaping the theater of modern identity.

Chapter 12: The Language of Online Presence

Being "online" is itself a form of body language. The green dot beside a name signals availability, presence, and sometimes obligation. It is a digital shadow that follows us everywhere.

Psychologists note that presence indicators create social pressure. To be online but unresponsive can feel like avoidance, while being offline can feel like withdrawal. These cues shape expectations of immediacy.

In friendships and relationships, online presence becomes a measure of intimacy. A partner's constant availability may be seen as devotion, while absence may trigger insecurity. The meaning depends on context and emotional stakes.

Online presence is not neutral. It is a signal of attention, shaping how trust and intimacy are negotiated in the digital age.

14

Chapter 13: The Semiotics of Profile Pictures

Profile pictures are the faces of digital identity. They are chosen carefully, signaling mood, personality, and intent. A smiling photo may suggest openness, while a serious one may project authority.

Linguistically, profile pictures function as symbols. They condense identity into a single image, shaping how others interpret and engage. The choice of picture is itself a form of communication.

Psychologically, profile pictures allow individuals to control perception. They can mask insecurity, project confidence, or signal belonging. The act of updating a picture is a gesture of reinvention.

Profile pictures are digital masks. They reveal and conceal, shaping how intimacy and trust unfold in virtual spaces.

15

Chapter 14: The Currency of Shares and Retweets

Sharing content is a gesture of endorsement. It signals alignment, humor, or solidarity. A retweet or share is not just replication but participation in a digital conversation.

Psychologists note that sharing reflects social identity. People share content that reinforces their values, beliefs, or affiliations. The act of sharing becomes a ritual of belonging.

In relationships, shares can be intimate. Sending a meme to a partner can signal affection, while sharing an article can spark dialogue. The gesture is both playful and serious.

Shares and retweets are digital currency. They measure influence, shape discourse, and reveal the networks of attention that define modern culture.

16

Chapter 15: The Language of Group Chats

Group chats are microcosms of digital society. They reveal hierarchies, alliances, and rhythms of interaction. The frequency of replies, the use of emojis, and the timing of responses all shape group dynamics.

Psychologists note that group chats amplify social pressure. Silence can be interpreted as exclusion, while constant replies can signal dominance. The digital body language of groups is complex and layered.

In friendships, group chats can strengthen bonds. In professional contexts, they can expose tensions. The act of participating is itself a negotiation of belonging.

Group chats are digital communities. They reveal how intimacy, conflict, and humor coexist in the compressed space of screens.

Chapter 16: The Digital Handshake of Replies

Replies are the handshakes of digital communication. They confirm acknowledgment, signal respect, and shape the rhythm of dialogue. A quick reply can feel warm, while a delayed one can feel cold.

Psychologists note that replies trigger reciprocity. Humans are wired to respond to acknowledgment, and the absence of reply can feel like rejection. Replies are not neutral; they carry emotional weight.

In relationships, replies are measures of care. A partner's attentiveness in replying can strengthen intimacy, while neglect can erode trust. The meaning depends on context and expectation.

Replies are digital gestures of presence. They shape how trust, intimacy, and respect unfold in the virtual age.

18

Chapter 17: The Future of Digital Body Language

Digital body language is evolving. New platforms, new cues, and new rhythms will reshape how we communicate. The rise of AI, augmented reality, and immersive spaces will create new grammars of presence.

Psychologists predict that digital cues will become more embodied. Avatars, gestures, and haptic feedback will blur the line between physical and virtual. The body will extend into digital space.

In relationships, this evolution will reshape intimacy. Virtual gestures will carry emotional weight, creating new forms of closeness and conflict. The meaning of presence will expand.

The future of digital body language is not just about technology but about humanity. It will reveal how deeply we crave connection, and how we reinvent language to satisfy that need.

www.ingramcontent.com/pod-product-compliance
Lightning Source LLC
Chambersburg PA
CBHW062309240926
51846CB00013B/935
9782748966220